1 **CORINTHIANS** CHALLENGE TO MATURITY

STUDIES IN THIS SERIES

Available from Marshall Pickering

1 corinthians

CHALLENGE TO MATURITY

16 DISCUSSIONS FOR GROUP BIBLE STUDY
BY MARILYN KUNZ AND CATHERINE SCHELL

small group bible studies

Marshall Pickering

Marshall Morgan and Scott
Marshall Pickering
3 Beggarwood Lane, Basingstoke, Hants RG23 7LP, UK

Copyright © 1973 by Neighborhood Bible Studies Inc.
Originally published in the US by Neighborhood Bible Studies Inc.
First published in the UK in 1987 by Marshall Morgan and Scott
Publications Ltd
Part of the Marshall Pickering Holdings Group
A subsidiary of the Zondervan Corporation

British Library CIP Data
1 Corinthians.– (Small group Bible studies)
  1. Bible.N.T. Corinthians, 1st– Commentaries
  I. Series 227′.207   BS2675.3

  ISBN 0-551-01442-3

Printed in Great Britain by
Eyre & Spottiswoode Ltd, Portsmouth, U.K.

contents

How to Use
This Discussion Guide

Sharing leadership—why and how

Each study guide in the Small Group Bible Study series is prepared with the intention that the ordinary adult group will by using this guide be able to rotate the leadership of the discussion. Those who are outgoing in personality are more likely to volunteer to lead first, but within a few weeks it should be possible for almost everyone to have the privilege of directing a discussion session. Everyone, including people new to the Bible who may not yet have committed themselves to Christ, should take a turn in leading by asking the questions from the study guide.

Reasons for this approach are:

1/ The discussion leader will prepare in greater depth than the average participant.

2/ The experience of leading a study stimulates a person to be a better participant in the discussions led by others.

3/ Members of the group which changes discussion leadership weekly tend to feel that the group belongs to everyone in it. It is not "Mr. or Mrs. Smith's Bible study."

4/ The Christian who by reason of spiritual maturity and wider knowledge of the Bible is equipped to be a spiritual leader in the group is set free to *listen* to everyone in the group in a way that is not possible when leading the discussion. He (she) takes his regular turn in leading as it comes around, but if he leads the first study in a series he must guard against the temptation to bring a great deal of outside knowledge and source material which would make others feel they could not possibly attempt to follow his example of leadership.

For study methods and discussion techniques refer to the first booklet in this series, *How to Start a Small Group Bible Study*, as well as to the following suggestions.

How to prepare to participate in a study using this guide

1/ Read through the designated section of 1 Corinthians daily during the week. Use it in your daily time of meditation and prayer, asking God to teach you what he has for you in it.

2/ Take two or three of the guide questions each day and try to answer them from the passage. Use these questions as tools to dig deeper into the passage. In this way you can cover all the guide questions before the group discussion.

3/ As an alternative to using this study in your daily quiet time, spend at least an hour in sustained study once during the week using the above suggestions.

If you prepare well for each study session, you will find that this letter has much to challenge, strengthen and mature you in your spiritual life. It deals with many issues of particular interest and concern to Christians in our generation.

How to prepare to lead a study

1/ Follow the above suggestions on preparing to participate in a study. Pray for wisdom and the Holy Spirit's guidance.

2/ Familiarize yourself with the study guide questions until you can rephrase them in your own words if necessary to make you comfortable using them in the discussion.

3/ If you are familiar with the questions in the guide, you will be able to skip questions already answered by the group from discussion raised by another question. Try to get the movement of thought in the whole chapter so that you are able to be flexible in using the questions. Most of the discussions will require only one session, especially if everyone comes well prepared.

4/ Pray for the ability to guide the discussion with love and understanding. Pray for the members of your group during the week preceding the study you are to lead.

How to lead a study

1/ Begin with a short prayer asking God's help in the study. You may ask another member of the group to pray if you have asked him ahead of time.

2/ Have the Bible portion read aloud by paragraphs (thought units), not verse by verse. It is not necessary for everyone to read aloud or for each to read an equal amount.

3/ Guide the group to discover what the passage says by asking the discussion questions. Avoid going woodenly through the study using each and every question. The group will often answer two or three questions in their answers to and discussion of one question. Omit those questions already answered. If you cannot discern the meaning of a question, don't use it, or else say to the group that you don't understand the question but they might. If they find it difficult, leave it and try simply to find the main point of the Bible paragraph.

4/ Use the suggestions from the section on *How to encourage everyone to participate*.

5/ Encourage everyone in the group to be honest in self-appraisal. If you are honest in your response to the Scripture, others will tend to be honest also.

6/ Allow time at the end of the discussion to answer the summary questions which help to tie the whole study together.

7/ Bring the discussion to a close at the end of the time allotted. Close in a prayer relevant to what has been discussed. Each session should run from an hour to an hour and a half. On those discussions which may take more than one session, this is indicated at the beginning of the study. It is *not* recommended that you spend more than two sessions on one chapter.

How to encourage everyone to participate

1/ Encourage discussion by asking several people to contribute answers to a question. "What do the rest of you think?" or "Is there anything else which could be added?" are ways of encouraging discussion.

2/ Be flexible and skip any questions which do not fit into the discussion as it progresses.

3/ Deal with irrelevant issues by suggesting that the purpose of your study is to discover what is *in the passage*. Suggest that tangential or controversial issues be discussed informally after the regular study is dismissed.

4/ Receive all contributions warmly. Never bluntly reject what anyone says, even if you think the answer is incorrect. Instead ask in a friendly manner, "Where did you find that?" or "Is that actually what it says?" or "What do some of the rest of you think?" Allow the group to handle problems together.

5/ If a question arises in the discussion about which there seem to be two or three possible answers in the passage, state these answers as the group finds them and then let the matter drop. There are some issues which have not been settled through hundreds of years of church history and your discussion group won't settle them in an hour. It is not always necessary to settle on one final answer to a question. Some of the guide questions are thought questions and do not have one single answer.

6/ Be sure you don't talk too much as the leader. If possible, redirect those questions which are asked you. A discussion should move back and forth between members of the group, not just between the leader and the group. The leader is to act as moderator and guide for the day.

7/ Don't be afraid of pauses or silences. People need time to think about the questions and the Bible passage. Try not to answer your own question—either use an alternate question or move on to another area for discussion. After the group has given their answers to a question you may add your comments if they don't duplicate what has already been said.

8/ Watch hesitant members for an indication by facial expression or body posture that they have something to say, and then give them an encouraging nod or speak their names.

9/ Discourage too talkative members from monopolizing the discussion by specifically directing questions to others. If necessary speak privately to the over-talkative one about the need for discussion rather than lecture in the group and enlist his aid in encouraging all to participate.

Introduction to 1 Corinthians

BACKGROUND OF THE LETTER:

Corinth, a rich commercial seaport, was located on the narrow neck of land connecting central and southern Achaia (now Greece). A number of trade routes met there, making it a natural stopping place on the way from Rome to the East. The city had been destroyed by the Romans about 200 years before Paul's first visit, then reconstructed by Julius Caesar in 44 B.C. and given the status of a Roman colony. As the administrative capital of the province of Achaia, it was the seat of the Roman governor. Corinth's population during the first century A.D. was a mixture of Romans, Greeks, and many Eastern races including Jews. It numbered about a half million, with the ratio of two slaves to every free man.

Because of Corinth's central location and large mobile population, anything preached there soon spread to surrounding districts. Corinth was noted for its sexual license encouraged by the temple of Aphrodite, goddess of love, located on a hill above the city. Not only did the city have a reputation for moral corruption but it was luxury-loving and self-indulgent with a tendency to intellectual pride.

Paul had visited Corinth on his second missionary journey arriving probably the autumn of A.D. 50 (Acts 18:1-18). The founding of the church there was opposed by the Jews, but God encouraged Paul with the promise of his protection and the declaration that he had many people in that place. Paul stayed a year and a half on that first visit. Apollos, an eloquent preacher from Alexandria, came later to Corinth, strengthening and extending the young church (Acts 18:24—19:1).

OCCASION OF THE LETTER:

Paul wrote this letter from Ephesus sometime between A.D. 55

and 57 on his third missionary journey. He had heard reports of troubles in the Corinthian church, and also the Corinthian Christians had written him a letter asking questions about marriage, celibacy, food offered to idols and probably also the matters of public worship and spiritual gifts.

Discussion 1 / 1 Corinthians 1

The Source of Your Life

INTRODUCTION

Literary critics are often presumptuous in describing an author's emotions, but it does not seem unrealistic to suggest that of all Paul's letters this was the most difficult to write. It is harder to write to a son who has been expelled from college than to a son who has made the dean's list. Paul was not one to avoid unpleasant issues, and early in this letter he begins to point out the faults of the Corinthian Christians, his spiritual children in the Christian faith.

1 Corinthians 1:1-3

1. How does Paul establish his authority to write to the Corinthian church? How does he describe their relationship to Jesus Christ? In what way does Paul show that these Christians belong to a greater fellowship?

2. From this paragraph, what do all Christians have in common? What does it mean "to call on the name of the Lord Jesus Christ?" See also Acts 2:21.

1 Corinthians 1:4-9

3. For what reasons does Paul give thanks to God for these Corinthian Christians? In what ways is God's grace expressed in their lives?

4. For what future event do Christians, then and now, wait?

5. What is revealed about God in verses 4 through 9?

6. What things are past (accomplished), present, and fu-

ture for these Christians? What practical difference do these things make in *your* life?

1 Corinthians 1:10-17

7. After his salutation and a prayer of thanks, Paul presents one of the main reasons for his letter. What is Paul's plea? What has been happening among the Christians at Corinth?

8. What decisive answer does Paul give to these divisions (verses 9, 13)? According to the questions in verse 13, what wrong emphasis and thinking have become prevalent among the Christians at Corinth? What have they forgotten? Why must a loyalty to Paul or any other spiritual leader be secondary always to one's commitment to Christ?

9. If Paul were writing verse 12 today, what similar divisions among Christians in our country might he mention?

10. From verses 14-17 and also Acts 18:1-18a, what picture do you get of Paul's previous ministry in Corinth? Why is he now thankful that he was not involved in baptizing many people? What was Paul's mission among the Corinthians? Paul's message?

11. Why, do you think, do many Christians become confused about whom they are following? What can help to keep a person from falling into such confusion?

1 Corinthians 1:18-25

12. What two attitudes are possible toward the message of Christ's death on the cross? What spiritual state is true of those who hold each attitude? What is your attitude toward the message of the cross?

13. Why is the cross the central message of Christianity? See also Romans 3:23-25a; John 1:29; John 3:14, 15; Mark 10:45.

14. Read Isaiah 29:9-14 to discover the context of the Old Testament warning to which Paul refers in verse 19. What is the reason even highly educated people cannot understand the word of the cross? See verse 21.

15. What is the folly (nonsense) which Paul preaches? Why would both Jewish scholars and Greek debaters find it unpalatable? What do the Jews demand as the avenue to truth? the Greeks?

16. Where do you look for truth today—in miracles, in philosophical arguments, or in the death of Jesus Christ?

17. What is Paul's answer for those who seek a visible expression of God's power? What is his answer for those who want a rational understanding of God?

18. How does Paul remind his readers, Jews and Greeks, that their concept of God is too small?

1 Corinthians 1:26-31

19. For the most part the Corinthian Christians are very ordinary people. Why has God chosen them to know him? Why doesn't the Lord want people to put confidence in worldly wisdom, worldly strength, or worldly prominence?

20. Compare verse 29 with Ephesians 2:8, 9. What is man's proper attitude in the presence of God?

21. What is Jesus Christ to the Christian? Define the terms: wisdom, righteousness, sanctification, redemption. What, then, are we without Christ? See also Jeremiah 9:24.

SUMMARY

1. What two major points does Paul make in this chapter?

2. Why are these two issues important today for Christians?

3. From this chapter, what have you learned to help you avoid causing divisions among Christians? to help you heal breaches in a Christian group?

4. Ask each person in the group to make one statement which boasts of what the Lord has done for him.

Discussion 2 / 1 Corinthians 2

The Mind of the Lord

INTRODUCTION

In chapter one Paul indicated his disapproval of the dissensions among the Corinthians over their favorite preachers. He rejected human eloquence and wisdom as useful in knowing God since God's power and wisdom run contrary to men's view of these things. Christ's death on the cross, considered weakness and foolishness by men, is the way to come to know God and his power.

1 Corinthians 2:1-5

1. What was Paul's reason for coming to the Corinthians? Between what two ways of preaching did Paul choose? How did his choice affect his preaching in manner? in outcome?

2. What is our purpose in communicating the gospel to others? What methods are appropriate?

3. What was the central message Paul sought to convey? Why? What impressions do you think that people have today about what the central message of the church is?

4. What, do you think, caused Paul's feelings of weakness, fear, and trembling when he came to the Corinthians? If he did not doubt the validity of his message, about what did he have fears?

5. What qualities of personality do you find most persuasive in a person who seeks to convince you of something?

6. Upon what does your faith rest? If you are a Christian, how did you come to put your faith in Jesus Christ the Crucified?

7. What indicates that Paul suits his teaching to the present capacity of those whom he teaches? See also Mark 4:33. Why are some doctrines unsuitable for sharing with the spiritually immature?

8. How did the Lord Jesus handle inappropriate questions? See Acts 1:6-8; Mark 12:23-27. How can we follow Paul's pattern in verse 2 when someone wants to talk about "really fascinating questions"? As a Christian, what do you *know* which you can share?

9. What is the nature (verses 7-10) and purpose (verse 12) of the wisdom which Paul imparts to the mature?

10. What do you learn about the "rulers of this age (world)" from this paragraph? What kind of wisdom do the rulers of our age have?

11. Describe the most beautiful, awe-inspiring sight you have ever seen in nature (God's visible handiwork). Then read verse 9 again. What do you learn of God's plan? For whom is it prepared?

12. How does Paul come to know the "secret and hidden wisdom of God" (verse 7)? See verses 10 and following. Who, besides Paul, can understand this wisdom of God? How?

13. What does the Spirit of God help us to understand? What gifts does he bestow? See also Romans 5:15-17.

(Note—More on the gifts of the Spirit will be considered in chapter 12.)

1 Corinthians 2:14-16

14. In contrast to those who possess the Spirit (verse 13), how does Paul describe the person in verse 14? What are the reactions of this man to the gifts of God's Spirit? Why?

15. What do you learn about the spiritual man from verse 15? What responsibility does he have concerning spiritual truths (verse 13) and spiritual gifts (verse 14)?

16. How are the two seemingly contradictory thoughts of verse 16 both true? See also John 7:15-17; 14:23; 15:15.

SUMMARY

1. Why is man's wisdom in conflict with God's wisdom?

2. List all the main verbs in verses 10-16. With what area of a man's life mainly do they deal? What indicates that the issue is not between earthly wisdom and heavenly emotion? How is a Christian called upon to use his mind?

3. From this chapter what is the one indispensable requirement for understanding the wisdom of God?

Discussion 3 / 1 Corinthians 3

God's Temple

INTRODUCTION

In chapter two Paul reminded the Corinthians who had become Christians through his preaching that they have responded to the gospel message preached in God's power, not in man's eloquence. He told them that it is impossible for men to understand the thoughts of God or the gifts of God without possessing the Spirit of God.

1 Corinthians 3:1-4

1. What is Paul's analysis of the spiritual maturity of these Corinthian Christians? How has this affected his ministry among them?

2. What are the indications of immaturity in a Christian? What are the Corinthian Christians jealous about? What are they arguing about?

3. How can we be deceived into thinking ourselves spiritually mature if we argue over the teaching emphasis of particular teachers or spiritual movements to which we belong? How should the spiritually mature person behave concerning these issues?

1 Corinthians 3:5-9

4. What picture from daily life does Paul use to illustrate his and Apollos' ministry? How is their work complementary? Without what is their work worthless? What is the unique work God performs in a life?

5. Paul moves from describing the Corinthian Christians as God's field in which he and Apollos have labored as farmers to picturing them as a building under construction which belongs to God. Find at least four things Paul says about his work as a pioneer missionary.

6. What does Paul mean that Jesus Christ is the foundation? For what? Why is any other basis futile?

7. What different types of material do men use to build on the foundation of Jesus Christ? How and when will all men's works be evaluated? What does this suggest about the impropriety of *our* evaluating another person's work for the Lord?

8. What concern are we to have about our own work? How does Paul indicate that our work as a Christian does not affect our eternal salvation? See also Ephesians 2:8-10.

1 Corinthians 3:16-17

9. Notice in verse 16 the further description of God's building (verse 9). What is the purpose of a temple?

10. Contrast Paul's statement about the Corinthian Christians in verses 1-3 and his tremendously challenging declaration in verse 16. How can both be true? Consider the depth of meaning associated with the word *temple* for Paul as a Jew. See Exodus 25:8; Ezekiel 37:27-28.

11. As you read verse 17, keep in mind that Paul is speaking of the whole group of Christians at Corinth as God's building, God's temple. What warning does he give in verse 17? For whom is this warning meant? See chapter 1:10-12; 3:3-4. What difference will this study make in your attitudes and actions toward the local groups of Christian believers in your town?

1 Corinthians 3:18-23

12. In the context of chapters 1 through 3, what self-deception is Paul talking about in verses 18-20?

13. What sorts of things would you say characterize the

wisdom of this world today? What, for example, does current advertising tell us is *wise?*

14. What does it mean to "boast of men" (verse 21)? How have the Corinthian Christians been guilty of this? To what extent are you guilty of this? Who are the "Pauls", "Apolloses" and "Cephases" of our day about whom Christians boast? Why do we do this?

15. Compare 1:31 and 3:21. When is boasting acceptable? According to verses 21b-23, why is boasting of men unsuitable and illogical? Why don't Christians need to limit themselves to a particular teacher or group? What belongs to every Christian (verses 21b, 22)? Explain. To whom does each Christian ultimately belong (verse 23)?

SUMMARY

1. What applications can you make from this chapter for the Christian today? To what weaknesses are you prone? How, specifically, can you avoid the errors pointed out here?

2. In society as a whole it is the immature person who follows and worships movie stars, musical groups, etc. In Christian circles it is the immature Christian who makes celebrities out of those whom he should consider God's "servants through whom (he) believed" (verse 5). From this chapter, what is the proper way to appreciate spiritual leaders?

3. Close with prayers of thanks for God's servants and builders we have today. Ask the Lord's help for them in their ministry. Ask forgiveness for viewing them inappropriately.

Discussion 4 / 1 Corinthians 4

Fools for Christ's Sake

INTRODUCTION

In the previous chapter Paul warned the Corinthian Christians that their quarrels are an evidence of their spiritual immaturity. He stressed the fact that he and Apollos are both God's servants, assigned their tasks by the Lord. The Corinthian church is depicted as God's field in which Paul and Apollos plant and water, and as God's temple in which Paul lays the foundation of Christ on which other craftsmen must build.

1 Corinthians 4:1-5

1. How should the Corinthian Christians regard their spiritual leaders? By definition, what are *servants* and *stewards* supposed to do?

2. What is the responsibility of those who are God's stewards? How does Paul view the problem of whether he is doing what other people expect of him? Why doesn't he worry about this?

3. When, by whom, and on what evidence will every man be judged? Why can't we adequately judge the work of another Christian, or even our own work?

1 Corinthians 4:6-7

4. For what purpose has Paul used Apollos and himself as illustrations? What does Paul want the Corinthians to do? What is to be the rule for their living as Christians?

5. Why is being proud of one leader and disparaging of another so wrong for Christians? Why is the Lord alone worthy of our enthusiasm? See also Exodus 20:3-5.

6. What does Paul intend to bring out by his three questions in verse 7? What possessions or abilities do some Christians tend to brag about?

1 Corinthians 4:8-13

7. List in two columns the tremendous contrast Paul draws (verses 8-13) between the apostles' situation and that of the Corinthian Christians.

8. According to verse 8, what has happened to these Corinthians since they became Christians? From whom did they receive all this? What lack does Paul see in them which he longs that they overcome? Why (verse 8)?

9. Share your own experience of longing for spiritual maturity in another. How does spiritual immaturity affect our fellowship with other Christians?

10. What experiences has God allowed his apostles to have (verses 9-13)? Compare verses 11, 12 with Paul's experiences in Acts 9:15, 16, 23-25; 14:19, 20; 16:22-24; 17:32.

11. Instead of going through the difficulties Paul has been facing, what is the Corinthians' situation?

12. According to verse 11, what is Paul's situation even as he is writing to them? What are Paul's priorities in life? What choices has he made which have resulted in these things happening to him? Why is he a "fool" (verse 10)?

13. What attitudes do the apostles exhibit toward those who are against them? To what degree can you say that these are your attitudes?

14. How does Paul define (verse 13) the "spectacle" he mentions in verse 9? In contemporary terms, how would you put what Paul is saying?

1 Corinthians 4:14-21

15. Why does Paul remind the Corinthians of all that has

happened and is happening to him? Why, perhaps, should they feel ashamed?

16. What unique claim does Paul have on these Christians (verse 15)? Is Paul now contradicting all that he has been saying in this letter about not quarreling over which leaders to follow? If not, why not?

17. Imagine the emotions of love, frustration, anger, sympathy, and tenderness with which a father might write to his wayward child. How does Paul express each of these emotions (verses 14-21)? What does he beg them to do? What does he threaten (verses 18-21)? Remember that Paul has described himself as their father in Christ.

18. What is Timothy's job to be? What contrasts between Timothy and the Corinthians may be suggested by the description of verse 17?

SUMMARY

1. Chapters 1-4 form the first major division of this letter. What would you say is Paul's chief concern?

2. Is the immaturity of the Corinthian Christians caused by their attitude toward their leaders, or does their immaturity cause them to have the party spirit for various leaders or groups?

3. From these chapters, what do you learn about Jesus Christ?

4. Discuss how to avoid divisions between believing Christians and how to heal any divisions which have occurred because of an emphasis on one doctrine or another. Deal with this question as between individuals, not denominations.

Discussion 5 / 1 Corinthians 5

Immorality among You

INTRODUCTION

In chapter four Paul presented his credentials for writing to the Corinthian Christians as a father. He reminded them of what it cost him to preach the gospel, contrasting his situation to theirs, and warned them that he hopes soon to be with them. The implication is that they would be wise to correct what is wrong before his arrival.

1 Corinthians 5:1-5

1. To what problem does Paul now turn? Why was this particular case shocking even for Corinth, which was notorious in the ancient world for immorality? (Note—The woman was probably the man's stepmother, and since nothing about her is said, she was no doubt a pagan.)

2. What shocks Paul as much as the man's behavior? What attitude should the Christians at Corinth have had about this situation? What ought they to have done? How has a blasé attitude toward sin infected Christian circles today? Why is this attitude so dangerous?

3. What is Paul's judgment in the matter? What does he say the Corinthian Christians must do? Why does this act call for Jesus' empowering? How does verse 2c help to explain the meaning of "deliver this man to Satan"? (How would casting the guilty man out of the fellowship of Christians, away from gatherings for prayer, preaching and the teachings of the gospel, mean turning him over to the influence of Satan?)

25

4. What indicates that this step is not vindictive? What effect is hoped for? What does this man need to realize about the seriousness of his sin? For an interesting parallel see Genesis 3:23-24.

1 Corinthians 5:6-8

5. What attitude do the Corinthian Christians apparently have about this situation? What don't they realize about the effect of sin within their fellowship? What warning does Paul give by comparing this sin to leaven (yeast)?

6. What effects has the general immorality in our society had on the Christian church today? How should the church today deal with the problems of immorality in the lives of its members?

7. What instructions does Paul give (verses 7, 8)? Note—Paul uses the Passover ritual as an illustration. Before the Passover feast began, the householder would search out and remove all fermenting material from the premises. During the 7 to 8 days of the feast, only unleavened bread would be eaten. (For background on the Passover, see Exodus 12:1-36.)

8. Because Christians are a new batch of unleavened dough, what are they to do with the leaven of sin? In a way, Paul is telling the Christians to *be* what they *are*. How can this apply to us today?

9. The Passover was an occasion for celebration and festival. By referring to the Passover, what is Paul saying should be the atmosphere of the Christian life?

10. How have the Corinthian church's actions, or lack of action, thus far in this situation failed to be a response of purity and truth? (Note—Although this man remained in their midst, the truth was that he was not in their fellowship, not in fellowship with the Lord.) See also 1 John 1:3, 6, 7.

1 Corinthians 5:9-13

11. What were Paul's instructions in a previous letter? How does he clarify what he meant? Why doesn't Paul call for

the church to remove itself from any contact with the world? See also Matthew 5:13-16; 28:18-20.

12. Define the six specific sins mentioned in verse 11. Why, do you think, are these particular sins mentioned? What is infectious about each? What makes these sins highly visible to the society at large?

13. Why does Paul say not even to eat with such a person? Why is Paul so strong on keeping the world out of the church, but not the church out of the world?

14. What responsibility do we as Christians *not* have? What responsibility *do* we have? What action is demanded?

SUMMARY

1. From Paul's teachings in this chapter, what would you conclude are the purposes of a local church fellowship?

2. Do you know of any church today where the instructions of this chapter have been ignored? Have been followed? What have been the results?

3. Why, do you think, does Paul insist that the Corinthian church take the responsibility of disciplining the man who is sinning, rather than admonishing him?

4. Close with David's prayer for forgiveness in Psalm 51: 1-12. Read aloud in unison if everyone has the same translation. If not, ask one person to read the passage aloud while everyone else uses the Psalm as a silent prayer.

Discussion 6 / 1 Corinthians 6

Do You Not Know?

INTRODUCTION

In the previous chapter Paul dealt directly and severely with a specific instance of immorality in the Corinthian church. He urged them to exclude from their fellowship any Christians who allowed the leaven of sin to permeate their lives. In this chapter he continues to admonish them on moral issues.

1 Corinthians 6:1-6

1. With what new area of concern does Paul now deal? What wrong choice has been made (verses 1, 4, 6)?

2. How does Paul set out to prove that it is unwise to take a lawsuit between Christians to the civil authorities (verses 2, 3)?

3. In what two areas will Christians some day be responsible to pass judgment? In comparison to that, over what areas should at least some Christians now be competent to judge matters properly? If any group of people ought to be skilled at judging right from wrong, why should it be Christians? (1 Corinthians 1:24b, 25, 30; 2:15, 16) What resource are the Corinthian Christians spurning by their actions?

4. How should Paul's repeated use of the word *brother* help them to understand what he is trying to teach them?

1 Corinthians 6:7-8

5. What further step in thinking does Paul seek to have his

readers take (verse 7)? What choice does he suggest is open to them? See also Matthew 5:39-41. How far have the Corinthian Christians moved from thinking in terms of the Sermon on the Mount? Like whom are they behaving?

6. Search your own heart and actions in the light of verses 7, 8. How can we escape thinking in terms of material success? How do we betray our real feelings?

1 Corinthians 6:9-11

7. For the third time in this chapter Paul raises the question "Do you not know?" in verse 9. What three things does Paul suggest that the Corinthian Christians do not know? How is it possible to have heard something but not really know it?

8. How should a fuller realization, a true knowledge, of verses 9 and 10 affect the attitudes and actions of these Christians? About what are they in danger of being deceived? To what extent do verses 9, 10 describe today's society? What are some of the pressures which can influence a Christian to think that the morals of such a society are right?

9. What is the difference between these Christians and the rest of the Corinthian community? What does verse 11 reveal about the transforming power of Jesus Christ? What three words does Paul use to describe the action God took to make these unrighteous people righteous? In what kinds of lives, to your knowledge, has God's power proven operative today?

1 Corinthians 6:12-20

10. What does Paul mean that "all things are lawful for me"? Comparing verse 12 with verses 9, 10, about what kinds of things is Paul not speaking in verse 12?

11. What two criteria are suggested for a Christian to use in making decisions (verse 12)? What two questions should a person ask himself about anything he considers doing?

12. How can the illustrations from verse 13 help us put our choices into a right perspective? Remember that Paul has already challenged his readers about some choices in verse 7.

13. What distinctions does Paul make about the uses of the

body (verse 13)? What two things await the body in the future? What event gives us confidence concerning our own resurrection?

14. Paul asks the question, "Do you not know?" three more times (verses 15, 16, 19). What conclusion does Paul draw from the fact that his body is a member of Christ (verse 15)? Why?

15. Contrast the two unions mentioned in verses 16, 17. What is the unique harm in the sin of immorality?

16. Discover at least three things Paul teaches about our bodies in verses 19, 20. Therefore, how ought the Christian to use his body? For the price by which the Christian has been bought, see 1 Peter 1:18, 19.

SUMMARY

1. The Corinthians have been concerned about wisdom and knowledge. Six times in this chapter Paul challenges his readers to live in the light of the reality which they should *know* (verses 2, 3, 9, 15, 16, 19). Summarize the conclusions you draw from answering Paul's series of questions.

2. Because of what has happened to you if you are a Christian (verse 11), how are you to live (verse 20)? Share specific ways you can glorify God.

Discussion 7 / 1 Corinthians 7

Remain As You Are

INTRODUCTION

In chapters 1-6 Paul wrote about things he had heard from others concerning the Corinthian Christians. In chapters 7 through 15, he deals with questions about which they themselves have written him. In this chapter he handles problems concerning marriage, circumcision, and slavery which were prompted by the fact that the people within the Corinthian church came from different backgrounds—Jewish, Greek, Roman.

(You may wish to discuss this chapter in two sessions. If so, plan to divide it after verse 24.)

1 Corinthians 7:1-7

1. What do you imagine is the Corinthians' question which prompts Paul's answer in verses 1, 2? With what practical reality does Paul deal? What does he recommend? In what ways does our society today present the individual with temptations to immorality?

2. What is the proper attitude toward sexual relationships between husband and wife? Who is in charge? What is taught about the cessation of sexual activity? What danger is to be considered?

3. What does Paul say about himself in this matter? How does he indicate his situation should not be a matter for pride?

1 Corinthians 7:8-11

4. In verses 8-11, Paul answers two questions—the first

applies to the unmarried, the second to the married. What seem to be the questions? What are Paul's answers?

5. In each case, what principles does Paul set forth? In each case, what qualifying circumstances and alternative solution are suggested?

6. What is Paul's teaching from the Lord on separation and divorce (verses 10, 11)? See also Mark 10:5-12 and Luke 16:18.

1 Corinthians 7:12-16

7. What new element in the marriage situation is introduced in this paragraph? What, apparently, are the questions which Paul is answering here?

8. What principles does Paul set forth in the situation where a Christian is married to an unbeliever? Why might the unbelieving partner not consent to live with the Christian? What does this imply about the revolutionized life of the Christian?

9. Why might the Christian believer be tempted to divorce an unbeliever? What tensions and problems can arise in this situation? (Note—Paul is speaking about those who are already married when one partner becomes a Christian. He is not dealing here with the question of a believer choosing to marry an unbeliever. Apparently even the Corinthians were not generally tempted to do this.)

10. What two reasons (verses 14, 16) are given for the believer not to seek to divorce the unbeliever? How can (should) living intimately with one who serves and loves the Lord Jesus be a blessing to the unbelieving partner? What advantage is it to the children?

11. In verse 15, just as he has throughout, Paul suggests an alternative, not as desirable, but under certain circumstances as the best thing to do. With what contingency does Paul deal in verse 15? What reason is given?

12. In closing this paragraph, what final challenge does Paul put to the believer? See also 1 Peter 3:12.

1 Corinthians 7:17-24

13. Although Paul has suggested various alternatives in the

issues discussed thus far in this chapter, what basic principle does he spell out in verse 17? What two things does this suggest about each person's life? How does this change your attitude toward the circumstances in your life?

14. What matters, and what doesn't matter, according to verses 18, 19? What question do you think prompted this answer? For why neither circumcision (the sign that the Jews were God's special people) nor uncircumcision counts now, see also Galatians 5:6; 6:14, 15. What principle is repeated in verses 20 and 24? See also verses 8, 10, 11.

15. Why doesn't it really matter for the Christian whether he has the social status of a free man or a slave? From what has the Christian slave been freed (Colossians 1:13, 14; Romans 6:6, 7)? Into what slavery has the free man entered when he becomes a Christian (Romans 6:17, 18)?

(If you discuss this chapter in two sessions, divide it at this point.)

1 Corinthians 7:25-31

16. Paul devotes the rest of the chapter to the reasons behind the answers he has given in verses 1-24. Why does Paul believe the unmarried should remain so?

17. Although Paul says that those who marry do not sin by marrying, what added problems will they have? In verses 29-31, what attitudes does he recommend? Why? Explain these attitudes in your own words. To what extent does your life reflect these attitudes?

1 Corinthians 7:32-35

18. What is Paul's desire for his fellow-Christians? What difference does marriage make in the use of a person's time and energies?

19. According to verse 35, what is Paul's motivation in all of what he says here?

1 Corinthians 7:36-40

20. What objections does Paul imagine? What freedom of

choice does he extend to his fellow-Christians? How does he follow the principle of verse 17 in his advice here?

21. How does the situation of Paul's day (verse 26) help you to understand his comment in verses 37, 38?

22. What final question does Paul handle in verse 39? What qualifications does Paul add to his answer of "yes"?

SUMMARY

1. "Remain as you are" (see verses 8, 11, 20, 24, 26, 40) is implied in other parts of this chapter also. Why, do you think, does Paul particularly emphasize this concerning one's marital state?

2. From the questions implied in this chapter, what insight do you get into the things the Corinthian Christians are involved in and concerned about?

3. We, like the Corinthian Christians, live in a sex-oriented and sex-obsessed society. From this chapter, what principles should be taught to young people and adults to give God's perspective on sex and marriage?

4. From this chapter, what is the Christian philosophy of marriage? of life? How does this contrast with the world's philosophy?

Discussion 8 / 1 Corinthians 8

Choices

INTRODUCTION

In the previous chapter, Paul answered questions concerning celibacy, marriage, divorce, circumcision and slavery. He turns now to other issues about which the Corinthians have asked him.

1 Corinthians 8:1-3

1. To what question which concerns the Corinthians does Paul now turn? (Note—This was a constant problem for Christians living in Greek cities.)

2. What wrong attitude toward this issue is Paul trying to bring to their attention? What's wrong with "knowledge" by itself? What other element is necessary in decision-making?

3. According to verse 2, what is incongruous about a person believing that he is completely aware and informed?

4. What is the basis of our communion with God? Why then is love a necessary factor for making judgments?

5. Although "food offered to idols" is not a problem for the majority of Christians today, what types of activities fall into the same category? To these the principles in this chapter should be applied.

1 Corinthians 8:4-6

6. What arguments apparently are set forth by those who feel it is right to eat food offered to idols? How does Paul feel about these reasons?

7. List the major points about God and about Jesus stated in verse 6. What distinction, if any, can you see between the activity of the Father and the Son as suggested by the phrases "from whom" and "through (or) by whom"?

1 Corinthians 8:7-13

8. What problem does Paul foresee in the application of this knowledge? What does he recognize about the background and spiritual immaturity of some of the Corinthian Christians? What could happen to them? Why?

9. How is a person's conscience defiled? See also Acts 24:16.

10. Why does eating (or not eating) have no spiritual value? What other things might fall into this category? See also Romans 14:1-6.

11. If these things are not important in themselves, on what basis should decisions about them be made? What is an important consideration?

12. To whom does Paul address this paragraph? How does he admonish them? See also Romans 14:13-16, 19-21.

13. In the illustration given in verse 10, what influence could a Christian have on others? With what result? Why would the same act harm one Christian but not the other? What knowledge does the weak Christian lack? What suggests that knowledge here means a strong inner conviction, not just having information?

14. Why should the more mature Christian condition his actions for the benefit of his less mature brother? What will he lose if he does this? But what may his brother suffer if he doesn't? How should a comparison of relative values for the people involved help us in our decision-making? How is this an expression of love?

15. What third person is always involved in any situation between two Christians? How is this in contrast to existential and situational ethics, which define ethics only in terms of self-expression and expediency?

16. What conclusion does Paul draw from what he has

considered in this chapter? What does he value in the expression of his own freedom?

SUMMARY

1. When does that which is right for us to do become sin? What practical guidelines would you suggest to help a person evaluate such situations?

2. From this chapter what conclusions can you draw about the similarities and the differences between Christians?

3. Share your reactions to the words of John Henry Jowett: "A vital part of all devotion is the remembrance of the goodness of God. Such a remembrance keeps my soul in the realm of grace. I am so inclined to proclaim my personal rights rather than glorify the favor of God, so inclined to exhibit my own prowess rather than God's most gracious bounty. And whenever I lose the sense of grace I become a usurper and take the throne."

Discussion 9 / 1 Corinthians 9

Rights and the Gospel

INTRODUCTION

In the previous chapter, Paul showed that the Corinthians' freedom to eat foods offered to idols (because they know that idols are not "real") must be voluntarily limited by a genuine concern for the conscience of their less knowledgeable Christian brothers. Now Paul turns to another matter in which he has rights but does not choose to use them.

1 Corinthians 9:1-2

1. What does Paul say about his position, experience, and unique relationship to the Corinthian Christians?

2. From verses 1, 2, what indication do you see of the things being said against Paul? How are the Corinthians themselves the validation of his credentials as an apostle of Christ?

1 Corinthians 9:3-7

3. From the questions he asks in this paragraph, what two problems has Paul faced?

4. What apparently was the practice of the other apostles regarding their financial support as they traveled and worked for the gospel?

5. What disadvantage is there to having Christian preachers and leaders hold regular jobs to earn a living?

6. What illustrations from everyday life does Paul use (verse 7) to point out the rightness of Christian workers expecting remuneration?

1 Corinthians 9:8-12a

7. What does the Old Testament teach about fairness to the laborer? How does Paul show that this applies to Christian workers (verses 9c, 10)?

8. What challenges does Paul put to the Corinthians (verses 11, 12a)? What answers does he expect? In what ways can we respond to those who serve us spiritually? What do we reveal about how we value spiritual things if we give much more reward to those who serve us in material things? How does this reflect upon us and not on the Christian minister or missionary?

1 Corinthians 9:12b-18

9. Why hasn't Paul exercised his right, his freedom, in this area? What is of supreme importance to him (verse 12b)? To what extent does such a priority of concern influence your decisions?

10. In case his refusal to accept material support would seem to weaken his argument that the Christian preacher deserves such assistance, how does Paul reinforce his argument from the Old Testament? from the Lord Jesus' own command? (See Matthew 10:9-11; Luke 10:7-8.)

11. From verses 15-18, what insight do you get into Paul's motives and value system? How strongly does he feel about not being paid? Why *does* he preach? What satisfaction does he have?

12. State what you understand to be the principle Paul lays down about this matter. What responsibility do the Corinthians have? What is Paul's personal preference? Why does he forego his "rights"?

1 Corinthians 9:19-23

13. What freedom has his decision in the matter of finances given to Paul? What has he chosen to do with this freedom (verse 19)?

14. What pattern of life does Paul follow and for what purpose?

15. In preaching the gospel, where does Paul start? Compare Acts 13:16, 17, 37-41 with Acts 17:22, 23, 30, 31. How and why does his approach differ?

16. How can we follow Paul's methods in sharing the gospel with another person? Why is it essential to know *where* a person is? What does Paul mean "to become weak"?

17. How would Paul define *happiness?*

1 Corinthians 9:24-27

18. To what training and discipline does an athlete submit? What are some of the corruptible crowns (perishable wreaths) for which athletes strive today?

19. In light of the things Paul has been speaking about in chapters 5—8, what point does he make about Christian conduct in verses 24, 25? In what areas have these Christians shown a lack of self-control?

20. What should motivate the Christian? See also 1 Peter 5:4 and Revelation 3:11.

21. What examples of self-control in his own life has Paul given the Corinthians? Why does he live as he does? What danger does he recognize?

SUMMARY

1. What responsibility do you have to those who serve you spiritually?

2. How do you reveal what is of importance to you? How do you personally use your time, energy, money, to indicate what you hold to be of ultimate value?

3. What spiritual exercises would help a Christian to run a good race?

Discussion 10 / 1 Corinthians 10

Idols

INTRODUCTION

In the previous chapter Paul spoke of his rights and duties as an apostle. He described his freedom as a Christian which he has exercised in choosing to preach the gospel at his own expense and in making himself the servant of Jew and Gentile in his manner of living. Paul's goal is to win as many as possible for the gospel. Through all of this, he disciplines himself spiritually so that he can win the crown that lasts forever.

1 Corinthians 10:1-5

1. In what experiences did all the Israelites share who were involved in the exodus from Egypt? See also Exodus 13:21; 14:21, 22, 29; 16:4, 35; 17:6. What attitude toward God should such experiences have produced in them?

2. What connection do you see between 9:27b and verse 5? Why cannot the Corinthian Christians assume that participation in Christian baptism and the Lord's Supper guarantees immunity from temptation or from judgment for deliberate disobedience and unfaithfulness?

1 Corinthians 10:6-13

3. As background for understanding Paul's Old Testament references in this section, before coming to the group discussion read Exodus 32:4-6; Numbers 25:1-9; 21:5, 6; 16:41-49. Of what sins does Paul say the Israelites were guilty (verses 7-10)? Which of these sins is social, directly involving other

people? How do the rest relate directly to our relationship with God?

4. Why is grumbling (verse 10) so bad? Against whom do we grumble? Why?

5. What functions do these lessons from history serve (verse 11)? What does Paul say should be our response to these lessons (verse 12)?

6. What contrast is there between verses 12 and 13? What type of person especially needs the warning of verse 12? What kind of person needs the promise of verse 13?

7. What four things do you learn about temptation from verse 13? What clear statement about God makes all the difference to the Christian who faces temptation? How do we and the Corinthians share the temptations of the Israelites?

8. Why, do you think, does God allow us to be tempted? Consider the opposite of each of the sins mentioned in verses 6-10. How is the temptation in each case also an opportunity for good?

1 Corinthians 10:14-22

9. On the basis of all he has said in verses 1-13, what command does Paul give (verse 14)?

10. When one partakes of the cup and the bread at the Lord's Supper, in what does he share (participate) when he eats and drinks (verses 16, 17)? What does the fact that those who participate in the Lord's Supper all eat from the one same loaf show about how Christians are related to one another?

11. What conclusion does Paul draw (verses 20, 21) from the parallel he describes between verses 16-18 and verse 19?

12. Although the idols are nothing (see again 1 Corinthians 8:4), what is the spiritual reality behind the pagan activities? (Note—Paul does not say that demons are nothing.)

13. In verse 21, what actions are incompatible? Why? How do the physical activities mentioned involve us in spiritual realities?

14. What will result if a Christian becomes partner in any way with demons (verse 22)? See Exodus 20:2-6; Deuter-

onomy 32:16-18. Why should a Christian take seriously the implication of his activities and associations?

1 Corinthians 10:23-30; 11:1

15. Read verse 23 aloud, the whole group reading the first phrase in each sentence and one person giving Paul's answer in the second half of each sentence. What must qualify all our actions as Christians?

16. Compare verse 24 with 8:9. How do we seek the good of our neighbor?

17. In verses 25-29, what three situations does Paul describe? What advice does he give in each case, and for what reasons?

18. How do verses 31-33 answer the questions in verses 29b, 30? What is the test for everything as far as our motivation is concerned?

19. Why may my actions, but not my conscience, be subject to another's conscience?

20. How far does a Christian's responsibility extend? Comparing verse 33 with verse 9:22b, in what way does Paul mean he tries to please all men in everything? Why is he doing this?

21. Describe ways in which a Christian today might try to live out verses 32, 33. Verse 11:1 seems to belong to this section. If so, in what areas is Paul calling upon the Corinthians to follow his example? How far should we follow Paul?

SUMMARY

1. What went wrong among the Israelites who had so many spiritual advantages? How is their experience a warning for us?

2. It was idols which tempted the Israelites, and idols hundreds of years later which presented a spiritual threat to the Corinthians. What "idols" threaten you as a Christian today?

3. From this chapter, list the criteria you can use to evaluate whether your motives and actions are to the glory of God.

Discussion 11 / 1 Corinthians 11

Appropriate Conduct

INTRODUCTION

Previous chapters have dealt with the personal choices of individual Christians. In chapters 11-14, Paul turns to the problems which have arisen in the early church in the conduct of their gatherings. It is essential that we discern the principles which underlie what Paul teaches the Corinthians so that we may see how they apply in the present day.

1 Corinthians 11:1-16

1. To what biblical principle does Paul refer to show the Corinthian Christians whether they should worship with veiled or unveiled head?

Note—The Jews, men and women, veiled their heads when praying. The Romans did also, but the Greeks sacrificed to their gods bare-headed. Members of the Corinthian church coming from these differing backgrounds would question what was the proper practice for them to follow.

2. How does the order of things spoken of in verse 3 affect what is appropriate in public worship? In both cases in verses 4, 5, what is to be avoided? Who is dishonored if the man covers his head when he prays in public? Who is dishonored if the woman fails to cover her head when praying in public?

Note—It was the harlot in first century Corinth who went about unveiled. For any woman in Corinth to go about unveiled would be to disgrace herself and her husband.

3. According to verse 7, whose glory is to be covered, and

whose glory is not to be covered?

4. What attitudes should both men and women express in their public worship? What are the reasons for decorum of dress among Christians, especially in their public worship? What does the use of words like *dishonor, disgraceful, degrading* and *proper* indicate?

5. In verses 8-12, what do you learn about the relationship between man and woman in the framework of creation?

6. What part is it assumed that both men and women will take in the public worship of the early church (verses 4, 5, 13)? How do you think Paul might address the church today in the light of general neglect in this area?

1 Corinthians 11:17-22

7. What picture do you get of the church gatherings at Corinth from this paragraph? What would happen to the fellowship between Christians in this atmosphere? How do discourtesy, selfishness and class distinction hinder fellowship in churches today? Give specific examples.

8. How can church activities be planned to develop true fellowship honoring to the Lord? According to verse 22, what are the results of what the Corinthians have been doing? Why don't they seem to realize what is happening? How, do you think, would they have described their get-togethers?

1 Corinthians 11:23-26

9. How does Paul describe the first Lord's Supper? What did the Lord Jesus do? What instructions did he give? What did the broken bread and poured out wine symbolize? What does the person who participates in the Lord's Supper remember (verses 24, 25) and proclaim (verse 26)?

10. In light of the stated purpose of the Lord's Supper (verses 25, 26), why is the Corinthian Christians' behavior (described in verses 17-22) so bad? Consider examples of ways in which the time and place of an action affects its morality.

11. What warnings and advice are given in verses 27-30? In verse 29 how does Paul explain the meaning of "in an unworthy (improper) manner" (verse 27)?

12. What judgment has come upon some of the Corinthian Christians because of their unworthy manner of participation in the Lord's Supper?

13. How can our attitude and demeanor at the communion table worthily (properly) reflect the significance of the Lord's Supper?

14. Why is *self-examination* important (verse 31)? Why does the Lord discipline us as Christians? What conclusion does Paul draw and what advice does he give (verses 33, 34)?

SUMMARY

1. Discuss what clothes, hair styles, degrees of make-up, jewelry, and body-language tell us about another person. What, do you think, should a Christian seek to express through these outward expressions of who he (she) is?

2. Fill in this outline from verses 25 and 26 with suggested scriptures, hymns, and sharing of personal experiences. (Perhaps you can use it for a church fellowship meeting.)

    1. Remember—all the things Jesus said and did.

    2. Proclaim the meaning of his death as the way of salvation for all.

    3. Wait—look for his return.

3. Close with prayers of remembrance and thanks for all the Lord Jesus has done for you.

Discussion 12 / 1 Corinthians 12

Spiritual Gifts

INTRODUCTION

In chapter 11 Paul treated the matter of appropriate dress for Christian women participating in public worship and the proper attitude and conduct of the Corinthian Christians at their gatherings to eat the Lord's Supper. Now Paul turns to the whole issue of the right use of spiritual gifts.

1 Corinthians 12:1-3

1. Trace the logical progression of Paul's thought in verses 1-3. How were the Corinthians deceived in their former pagan worship? (For "dumb" or "dead" idols, see Psalm 115:4-8.)

2. Since they seemed to be easily influenced, what basic test does Paul give them for the source of spiritual gifts? See also 1 John 4:1-3.

3. What does verse 3 suggest about what may have happened among them? What evidence do we have today that religious ecstasy may not always be Christian?

1 Corinthians 12:4-11

4. In what three categories is there to be variety (verses 4-6)? What may happen if Christians become intolerant of these variations?

5. In what must there be no variety? (What is "the same"?) Reflect again on the test given in verse 3.

6. What indicates (verses 5-7) these gifts are not given to individuals for their personal benefit? How should the gifts be used?

7. What is the invariable purpose of spiritual gifts (verse 7)? What responsibility does possession of a spiritual gift put upon the person who has it? If there is no expression of these gifts in a church, what questions should be asked?

8. To better understand what these gifts are, read from several translations the list of nine manifestations (gifts). Who is the source and distributor of all these gifts? How is a gift obtained? What, then, is an appropriate attitude toward receiving spiritual gifts? Toward different Christians having differing gifts?

1 Corinthians 12:12-13

9. What truths does Paul teach by his illustration in verse 12? How does a person become part of the body of Christ (verse 13)?

10. What differences dividing society in Paul's day are overcome in the oneness of Christ's body? See also Galatians 3:28; Colossians 3:11. If Paul were writing this letter today, what divisions in society would he say are overcome in the oneness of Christ's body?

11. Describe any experience you have had of the oneness of those in Christ.

1 Corinthians 12:14-26

12. What five things do verses 14-20 teach about the variety of spiritual gifts? How is the tendency to self-doubt on the part of one who does not have a particular gift handled?

13. In the light of the illustration used in this paragraph, what would happen if only one gift was given to all? If emphasis is laid upon one particular gift or ability, whose plan are we criticizing?

14. According to verse 21, to what is an attitude of superiority on the part of those who have a particular gift comparable? How can people be helped to get over such foolish attitudes? See also Proverbs 11:2; 16:18; Mark 7:21-23.

15. What is God's plan for the body? What do verses 22-24 imply about the value of the least person in Christ in his relation to the whole body? What happens in a local group of Christians if they violate the plan of the Lord as expressed in verse 25?

16. How is the reality of our unity emphasized in verse 26? Share examples of this suffering and this rejoicing together as Christians.

17. Note how Paul turns directly to the local church at Corinth ("you"). Put into your own words what verse 27 means. See also Ephesians 1:22, 23; Colossians 1:18.

18. How does God express his authority over what goes on in and through the church? What does the use of "first, second, third, then" seem to indicate? Define what you understand to be the work of each of the eight appointments mentioned. See also Ephesians 2:19, 20.

19. In the phrasing of the Greek language in which Paul wrote, it is clear that the expected answer to the questions in verses 29-30 is "no". How does this carry through the emphasis in verses 14-26 on inter-relationship and inter-dependence between Christians?

20. If the Lord chooses what the church needs and from whom, what ought to be our attitude toward spiritual gifts? Toward their expression and attainment?

21. What are the higher gifts? Although the lists in verses 28-30 are not completely parallel, in both listings which are the higher gifts and which are the lower? What direction ought this to give to our thinking and praying (verse 31)?

22. What does verse 31b suggest about the whole matter of spiritual gifts which greatly occupies the thinking of the Corinthians and that of many today? See also 1 Corinthians 14:1.

SUMMARY

1. What problems have the Corinthians apparently gotten into concerning spiritual gifts?

2. What does this chapter teach about the source, purpose, variety and priority of spiritual gifts?

3. How does man's desire to be independent from God and from his fellowman come to light in the way in which the Corinthians got the wrong idea about spiritual gifts? See also Genesis 3:4-6.

4. Since in Christ we are inter-dependent, ask each person to pray a sentence prayer of blessing for the person seated to his left.

Discussion 13 / 1 Corinthians 13

More Excellent

INTRODUCTION

It is important that this chapter be considered as a part, and in the context, of Paul's whole argument in chapters 11-14. In chapter 12, Paul taught that every believer has some spiritual gift with which he is to enrich the church; that these gifts, though varied in nature, are inspired by the same Holy Spirit. He taught that each member must function efficiently if the local church is to be healthy, and that some gifts, more important than others, are to be especially desired. Even better than the best spiritual gifts is a quality of life Paul praises in chapter 13.

1 Corinthians 13:1-3

1. What six possibilities does Paul suggest? How, in almost every case, is the extent of the act or gift emphasized? What three areas of life do these possible situations cover?

2. What is the result in each instance if the gift or act is exercised without love? Why do you think this is so? How does the motivation affect the true value of an act? See also 1 Corinthians 4:5; 1 Samuel 16:7.

3. How could the gift or the opportunity for the types of actions mentioned in verses 1-3 become a temptation? How can we test our motives?

4. Before reading the definition of love in the next paragraph, what is your definition of love? How could a person express love in each of the situations mentioned in verses 1-3?

1 Corinthians 13:4-7

5. Ask someone to read this section aloud substituting his

own name for "love". Then ask him to read it this way again, reading each definition the opposite of what is stated. Does reading it this way, or the way Paul wrote it, more nearly describe you? Why?

6. Why should the question perhaps be, not *what* is love, but *who* is love? Who is the best example of Paul's definition of love?

7. List in a column the series of words or phrases Paul uses to define love. Write opposite each a synonym, and note an incident from the Gospels in which Jesus expressed love in this way.

8. Taking the ten phrases in verses 4-7, ask different people in the group to take one phrase and mention briefly a situation in which that facet of love would be needed.

1 Corinthians 13:8-13

9. With what does Paul compare love (verse 8)? Why do these gifts have limited value while love is the greatest? See also 1 John 4:7, 8, 16.

10. What contrast does Paul draw between the present and the future (verses 9-13)? To what experience does he compare our life as Christians now and in the future (verse 11)? Of what immature attitudes and actions are the Corinthian Christians guilty? See, for example, 1 Corinthians 3:1-3; 8:9, 11.

11. What is the difference between "now" and "then" (verse 12)? Whom will we see "face to face"? (1 John 3:2) What will happen to all the things we haven't been able to understand?

12. Why do you think Paul reminds us that while we don't always understand now, God's knowledge of us is complete and we are fully understood by him? How should an awareness of this help you in your present situation?

13. In this life, faith and hope, as well as love, have an enduring quality. Why is love even greater than faith or hope?

SUMMARY

1. Review chapters 1-12, noting all the instances in which

it is clear that, although the Corinthians have many gifts, they are lacking in love.

2. Why is love not a gift? Who should have it? See also John 15:12, 17.

3. Share some of the facets of love to which you wish to give special attention as you continue to mature as a Christian.

Discussion 14 / 1 Corinthians 14

For Edification

INTRODUCTION

Having put the spiritual gifts of chapter 12 into the proper perspective of love in chapter 13, Paul returns to the problem of the Corinthians' emphasis on tongues. Read Acts 2:1-21; 10:44-48; 19:1-7 as background for this chapter.

1 Corinthians 14:1-5

1. Compare verse 1 with John 14:15. How do these two verses clarify what we should be doing as Christians? What attitude ought Christians to have toward spiritual gifts?

2. Why do you think one gift is especially singled out to be desired (verse 1)? What contrasts does Paul point out between speaking in tongues and prophesying in verses 2-4?
Note—*"Prophecy* in scripture includes foretelling future events, but more often refers to 'forthtelling' God's message in inspired words." (*New Bible Commentary*)

3. How could the three specific benefits of prophecy (preaching) help your church? If you were advising a seminary student, how would you suggest he develop preaching that builds up faith, that gives courage to face life, and gives hope?

4. Why is the one who preaches of greater value to the church than the one who speaks in tongues? According to verses 3-5, what is the way to judge the relative value of these spiritual gifts? What increases the value of tongues? Why?

5. What indicates that Paul is not speaking against tongues, but against the improper emphasis put on them by some?

6. What is Paul's argument (verses 6, 9)? How does he illustrate it from the field of music (verses 7, 8)? How is the lack of clarity dangerous (verse 8)?

7. Note and consider in verses 6-9 the progression of illustrations Paul uses—himself, musical instruments, the Corinthians. What does Paul desire in their speaking? What does he warn against?

8. How is lack of concern for others basic to most of the Corinthians' problems? How is it basic to their problem with tongues?

9. How does Paul continue his argument in verses 10, 11? How does lack of understandable communication create a barrier between people?

10. How does Paul seek to guide the Corinthians' enthusiasm for spiritual gifts (verse 12)? For the variety of spiritual gifts see again 1 Corinthians 12:7-11. If we followed Paul's guidance here, how would it move our emphasis away from ostentatious, perhaps self-centered, activity to that which benefits others? What can you do to help build up the church (your fellow-Christians)?

11. How would you sum up Paul's concern in this section?

1 Corinthians 14:13-19

12. Why should a person who speaks in tongues pray for the power to interpret (verses 13-17)? Why is it vital that our minds be involved in all that we do in our Christian meetings?

13. What do you learn about the gift of tongues itself in verses 13-16?

14. Although Paul himself speaks in tongues, what relative value does he put on tongues, especially as used in the church gatherings? Why?

1 Corinthians 14:20-25

15. What is Paul's plea in verse 20? How have the Corinthians been immature?

16. How, and for whose benefit, were tongues used on the day of Pentecost as described in Acts 2? According to 14:22, what is one function of tongues? How does Acts 2 verify this? On the other hand, what is the primary function of preaching (prophecy)?

17. What effect would hearing tongues spoken have on the outsider interested in Christianity who comes into a Christian gathering to learn more? What effect could preaching have on this person? What does the use of "everyone" and "all" in verses 23-24 tell you about first century church meetings?

(If studying this in two sessions, end first session here.)

1 Corinthians 14:26-33a

18. The first phrase of verse 26 may be translated, "What am I urging, then, brethren?" What types of contributions may be made to the group's worship? What should be the purpose or motive of these contributions?

19. What does verse 26 suggest about the worship experience of the early Christians? How does this differ from the worship service of your local church? What has the present-day church substituted for the sharing element in worship? What have we lost thereby?

20. What four rules does Paul give about speaking in tongues in group worship?

21. What rules are given for the prophets (inspired preachers or teachers)? For the purpose of prophecy, compare verses 3 and 31. What emphasis is repeated?

22. What truth about God does Paul give as the reason for the regulations he has suggested for their gatherings for public worship? What rules would Paul suggest for your church congregation to help them accomplish the purposes (verses 3, 24-26) a Christian gathering should serve? Would you need the rules he gave to Corinth or some quite different ones? Why?

23. What disciplines are set forth by the prophets?

24. Who may preach? What is the purpose? Compare verse 31 with verse 3. What emphasis is repeated?

25. What control do both the prophet and the speaker in

tongues have? Why must this control be exercised? (Verses 27, 32)

26. It may be assumed that the Corinthians have not always followed the rules laid down in verses 27-31. If they have not, what must have resulted? Which of these rules would be good ones for our Bible study discussions today?

1 Corinthians 14:33b-36

27. For the context of verse 34, see again 11:4, 5 and 14:26-33. Although women were expected to participate, how may things have gotten out of hand? Some translate "speak" (verses 34-35) as "chatter." How does this help to clarify Paul's intent here?

28. From verse 36, how are the Corinthians acting? What happens when any group of Christians begins to think this way?

1 Corinthians 14:37-40

29. What does Paul say about the instructions in this chapter that remove them from being just one man's opinion?

30. Read again verses 33a, 40. How can you personally develop habits of doing things decently and in order so that your Bible study and church group can function in a disciplined way? How can you begin to teach these principles in your home?

SUMMARY

1. Taking chapters 12, 13, 14 as a unit, list three or more major points made. How does each point apply today?

2. What principles applied from this chapter can help your Bible study group to function in a way that builds up, encourages, and strengthens everyone in it?

3. From this chapter it is easier, perhaps, to see what was wrong with the Corinthian church. What, however, by implication, was clearly *right* with the Corinthian church that is missing in many of our churches today?

Discussion 15 / 1 Corinthians 15

Resurrection

INTRODUCTION

It is possible that some in the church at Corinth were influenced by the current Greek ideas that when the soul (the real self) survived death by escaping the imprisoning body, it was either absorbed into the divine or lived on in a shadowy existence in Hades, the underworld. Any hope of *resurrection* was unthinkable to the Greek mind. Or it is possible that some may have thought the resurrection had already taken place (2 Timothy 2:18) and no future hope awaited Christian believers.

(You may wish to discuss this chapter in two sessions. If so, plan to divide it after verse 34.)

1 Corinthians 15:1-2

1. How have those to whom Paul writes responded to the gospel message he preached to them? What warning is implied in these verses? See also Acts 16:31; John 8:24; 6:40.

1 Corinthians 15:3-11

2. What is the core of the gospel as described in verses 3-4? Compare verse 3 with Isaiah 53:5-8, and verse 4 with Psalm 16:10. See also Acts 2:29-31.

Note—The very phrasing of verses 3-5 indicates a formulated creed that the early church used as a statement of belief. Paul says that what he delivered or passed on to them was what he had received.

3. How does Paul show that the resurrection was verified? (Verses 5-8) Consider the privilege of the Corinthians to be

able to meet such eyewitnesses. Through whom did you receive the witness of Christ?

4. Why is Paul's witness to the resurrection unique? How does Paul evaluate himself and his work? What has made the difference in Paul's life?

5. Define *grace*. How did the grace of God operate in Paul's life? How does it operate in your life?

6. What does Paul share with the other eyewitnesses and the apostles? What responsibility does everyone have who knows about the resurrection of Christ? How are you fulfilling your part? What is the purpose of preaching or telling? See also Romans 10:14.

1 Corinthians 15:12-19

7. What false teachings or doubts have come to the Corinthian church according to verse 12?

8. Count the number of "ifs" in this paragraph. What does this indicate about the type of writing Paul is using here? Write out the list of 11 conclusions (some repeated) which must be true if there is no resurrection of the dead.

9. Do you think the conclusion of verse 19 is valid? Explain. What does Christ's resurrection mean to us? See also Romans 8:11 and 1 Thessalonians 4:13-14.

1 Corinthians 15:20-28

10. Why need we not be in despair after reading verses 12-19? Review the proofs of Christ's resurrection mentioned in verses 5-8. What assurance does this give us concerning Christians who have died?

11. If you came to this earth from another galaxy in the universe and discovered this paragraph, what could you learn from it about human history from its beginning to its end? What things are past, what present, what future?

12. What details do verses 25-28 give of the event described in verse 24?

1 Corinthians 15:29-34

13. Although it is unclear today what the practice of being baptized for (on the behalf of) the dead meant, what is clearly the point of Paul's argument?

Note—Many think this was a proxy-baptism in which church members at Corinth were receiving baptism on behalf of Christian friends or relatives who had died before being baptized. Some think it refers to martyrdom for Christ. Since it can also be translated "baptized because of the dead" it could refer to the baptism of those influenced by the witness of a Christian who had recently died, and in hope of being re-united with him at the resurrection.

14. How might Paul live differently if he did not believe in the resurrection of the dead? How does a person's theology affect his way of life? See also Jesus' parable in Luke 12:15-21 and Romans 14:10-12.

15. According to verse 12, from whom have these doubts about the resurrection of the dead come? What influence do other people's ideas have on your thinking and then your conduct? Give several illustrations.

16. In verses 33, 34a, what challenge is given in light of the doubts which plague some of the Corinthians? According to verse 34b, what would some churches today share with the Corinthian church? When do you think doubting becomes sin? Remember Thomas' experience in John 20:24-29.

(If you discuss this chapter in two sessions, divide it at this point.)

1 Corinthians 15:35-41

17. What questions does Paul handle in this section of this chapter? Why does the fact that a person doesn't understand "how" sometimes keep him from belief? See also John 3:4, 9.

18. In verses 36-41, what illustrations from nature help to answer the questions in verse 35? What clues does this give you about the resurrection body?

19. How should Paul's emphasis on the creative power of God help those who have doubts about the resurrection of the body?

1 Corinthians 15:42-50

20. In what four ways is the resurrection body different from the body we now have (verses 42-44)? What are your emotions as you begin to grasp what this will mean?

21. List the contrasts between the first man Adam and the

last Adam? What do we receive from each Adam? See also Romans 5:17 and John 3:6. What do you learn from noting the verb tenses in verses 47-49?

22. Why cannot flesh and blood inherit the kingdom of God? What, then, is essential for a man to participate in God's kingdom?

1 Corinthians 15:51-58

23. Who will not die? What will happen to those who do not die? Why? When? At this time, what will happen to those who have died? See also 1 Thessalonians 4:13-18.

24. With verses 54-55, see verse 26. See also Isaiah 25: 8-9; Hosea 13:14; Daniel 12:2-3. When will these Old Testament prophecies be fulfilled?

25. Compare verses 50 and 53. Why does Paul use the imperative *must* in verse 53?

26. In verses 54-57, what will be the result of the change that has taken place in the living and the resurrected? Why have death and the grave had a sting and a victory? How are the sting and victory of death now overcome? See also 2 Corinthians 5:21; Romans 5:17; 6:23.

27. Paul concludes this great chapter with an exclamation of thanks and an exhortation to action. Why is the Christian's labor in the Lord's service not in vain? What responses does Paul call for on the basis of this truth? What does it mean to you to "abound in the work of the Lord"?

SUMMARY

1. Why is a correct understanding of the reality and the ramifications of the resurrection of the dead essential? What happens when our theology is weak in this area?

2. How has the emphasis of this chapter on the reality of the resurrection of the dead for all Christians (except those still alive at the Lord's return) enlarged your understanding, your faith, your commitment to Christ?

3. Assign individual final review topics as suggested on page 64. These can be presented following discussion of chapter 16, or can occupy a separate session.

4. Close the study with prayer, each person giving thanks for one of the things God has taught in this chapter.

Discussion 16 / 1 Corinthians 16

Personal Messages

INTRODUCTION

In the previous chapter Paul reached the climax of this letter in his great affirmation of the resurrection in 15:51-57. It is "the victory through our Lord Jesus Christ" which made this letter possible. It is also the reason why we are reading the letter nineteen hundred years later. In this closing chapter Paul turns to practical and personal matters.

1 Corinthians 16:1-4

1. What change do you observe in style and flavor between this section and chapter 15? Why must our theology always find expression practically?

2. What principles can you draw from this paragraph which are applicable to our giving as Christians today?

1 Corinthians 16:5-9

3. What are Paul's personal plans? On what basis does he seem to make his decisions?

4. Review briefly the major events described in Acts 19:1 —20:2. Why, do you think, are the two elements mentioned in verse 9 frequently coupled? What happens if a person serving the Lord emphasizes either fact in his thinking, neglecting the other?

1 Corinthians 16:10-12

5. What can you learn about Timothy by a little reading

between the lines here? See also 1 Timothy 1:2; 4:12, 14 and 2 Timothy 1:2, 6-8. How do you think Paul feels about him?

6. Why does the Lord use some men like Paul, others like Timothy, others like Apollos? How does he work redemptively through all personality types? Give examples today.

7. How does Apollos decide what to do? How could you be wrongly influenced by a strong Christian leader? What does Paul acknowledge with the "but" in verse 12? See also Psalm 37:23 and Proverbs 3:6.

1 Corinthians 16:13-14

8. Paul interrupts his personal messages with some exhortations. Paraphrase verses 13, 14 as you would if you were giving this advice to a young Christian. Why is each element needed in the Christian life?

1 Corinthians 16:15-18

9. The three people mentioned in verse 17 are apparently those who brought the questions from the Corinthians which Paul answers in the first part of this letter. Note, also, 1:16. What do you learn about these men? What does Paul urge concerning them?

10. What actions and attitudes are appropriate toward those who give themselves to the Lord's work?

1 Corinthians 16:19-23

11. For "the churches of Asia" (the province of Asia), see Acts 19:10, 26. Concerning Aquila and Priscilla, see also Romans 16:3-5; Acts 18:24-26. How does Paul's exhortation in verse 20 (as well as that in verse 14) encourage them to put aside their dissensions (1:11; 3:3)?

12. These last four messages (verses 21-24) Paul writes himself instead of dictating them. What strong warning does he give? How would you put 22a into a positive statement?

13. Compare 22b with Revelation 22:20, 21. The phrase used is "maranatha". How is it both a prayer and a promise?

Many believe these words were used by the early Christians as a password and greeting.

14. What final two things do the Corinthians receive with this letter?

SUMMARY

1. What impression do you get of the Christian activities going on in the early church throughout the Mediterranean world?

2. What practical expressions of love and fellowship in this chapter should you emulate in your churches and Christian fellowship groups today?

3. Close in prayer for those like the people mentioned in this passage who devote themselves to Christian service.

Discussion 17

Review of 1 Corinthians

Assign each member of the group at least one of the review topics. In Genesis 1, after a description of God's creative activity, we read "so God created man in his own image, in the image of God he created him; male and female he created them" (Genesis 1:27). One of the first characteristics to be observed about God is his creative power. Man in God's image has both the challenge and the opportunity to be creative.

In this Review, rather than just reciting the highlights of the chapters assigned to you, express something which you feel is important in them. Suggested modes: poetry, song, a poster, a banner (brown-bag), collage, prayer, essay, riddle, recipe, quiz, etc. You may wish to incorporate what you think are the verses of greatest import in your banner, etc.

Suggested topics for a review of this book are:

1. Chapters 1—4:   Wisdom
2. Chapters 5 and 6: Morality
3. Chapter 7:   Marriage
4. Chapters 8 and 9: Freedom
5. Chapter 10:   Temptation
6. Chapters 11—14:   Church
7. Chapter 15:   Resurrection